What Children Learn
In the Classroom

A Parents' Guide to Primary Education in England

Kate Stewart

Emerald Publishing
www.emeraldpublishing.co.uk

Emerald Guides
Brighton BN2 4EG

© Kate Stewart First edition 2008

ISBN 9781847160 78 2

Whilst every effort has been made to ensure that the information
contained within this book is correct at the time of going to
press, the author and publisher can take no responsibility for the
errors or omissions contained within.

I would like to express my thanks to everyone who has helped me in the writing of this book, and in particular to Paula Kingman who has been most generous in sharing her knowledge and expertise and who has been endlessly patient with my many, many questions.

This book is dedicated to all teachers
who work so hard and do such important work
and particularly to my mother,
Patricia,
who has taught me everything.

What Children Learn
In the Classroom

A Parents' Guide to Primary Education in England

They don't seem to 'do' Maths at school any more.

When my parents were young, they were taught the 'Three 'R's': Reading Writing and Arithmetic (...only one of which, of course, actually began with an 'R', but then it was a very long time ago!) In my day, we stopped all that, and instead we learnt English and Maths – with some Art and History thrown in if the teacher was keen on that sort of thing. That has all changed now.

Now, children in Primary School learn Literacy and Numeracy, Core Subjects and various other parts of the National Curriculum. This didn't bother me when my daughter started school. After all, 'A rose by any other name...' and all that. Surely, what she actually learnt would not have changed?

Not so. As an English graduate, I was flummoxed when her Year One teacher told me she could blend her phonemes. Was this good or bad? By year four she was Chunking. I was lost. How could I help her when I hadn't the faintest idea what her teachers were talking about? I watched her doing her homework. This wasn't what I had learnt when I was at school…

It has been a steep learning curve for me, especially as – when our son was diagnosed with Asperger syndrome at the age of 4 – we decided to take him out of school for part of the time and teach him ourselves. Suddenly, I *had* to be familiar with those wretched blended phonemes. I'm still working on the chunking.…

This book is a 'Cook's Tour' of what your child learns in school these days, as we steam towards the second decade of the twenty-first century. It will give you an idea of what to expect, a working knowledge of what is going on and the vocabulary to hold your own in parents' evenings. Most importantly, it will give you a window into your child's world. If you know what she is doing at school, you are well placed to help and support her, to encourage and assist, to know when to lavish praise and when to give a helping hand. If you have a basic understanding of what she is learning, you are in a position to let her teach you and to share the journey with her. Good luck!

Contents:

Chapter 1

How do they decide what to teach them at school?

Since 1996, all community and foundation schools, voluntary aided and voluntary controlled schools follow the National Curriculum. This sets out the subjects that are taught in schools, and to a certain extent decides the content of those subjects.

It is organised into parts, called 'Key Stages'. Those that affect pupils at primary school are Key Stage 1 (KS1), which involves Years 1 and 2 for pupils aged 5 – 7, and Key Stage 2 (KS2), which involves Years 3 – 6 for pupils aged 7 – 11. All pupils in KS1 and KS2 study the same subjects.

These subjects are the core subjects (Literacy, Numeracy and Science), and non-core foundation subjects (Design and technology (D & T), Information and communication technology (ICT), History, Geography, Art and Design, Music and Physical Education (PE).) There are also are non-statuary subjects (Personal, Social and Health Education (PSHE) and Citizenship, Religious Education and a Modern foreign language.)

For each subject, and for each key stage, the national curriculum sets out what pupils should be taught.

It also gives guidelines as to what children's expected attainment should be for that subject. Attainment is quantified by levels and is measured against attainment targets. These attainments targets describe what a pupil should, generally, be able to do in each subject in order to achieve each level. These levels are the same as those expressed in SATS (see chapter 7), so the progression of each pupil can be followed. It is also possible through this system for parents to be aware how their child is performing against national expectations, and even against other pupils. More importantly, it is possible to monitor how your child is attaining against his previous level, so that it should be possible to spot areas where your child is beginning to struggle before he gets into too much difficulty.

In KS1, between the ages of 5 and 7, the majority of pupils will be working between levels 1 and 3. In KS2, between the ages of 7 and 11, the majority of pupils will be working between levels 2 and 5. Within this, the expected attainment for the majority of pupils at the end of KS1 (age 7) is level 2 and at the end of KS2 (age 11) is level 4.

This then, gives the content of what is taught at school, and the level at which most children are likely to be working. A programme of study is published by the QCA (Qualifications and Curriculum Authority) to provide the basis for planning the scheme of work as delivered in schools.

National frameworks in literacy and mathematics exist to help teachers translate all of this consistently into practical, manageable lessons. Within all this structure, it is for the school to decide how it is going to teach the requirements of the national curriculum and how it will deliver against the expected standards. These decisions are usually communicated to parents in a number of ways – through the school prospectus, through open evenings, in a school development plan, through regular communication between head teacher, governors and parents. These decisions on how to implement the requirements of the national curriculum, together with other philosophies about learning and other experiences which the school offers, may be termed the School Curriculum.

The School Curriculum

The school Curriculum encompasses all learning, including that of the national curriculum, but also other learning and experiences that the school provides for its pupils. It should promote children's spiritual, moral, social and cultural development and prepare them for the opportunities, responsibilities and experiences of life. As such it must include a set of values, a statement of which was made by the National Forum for Values in Education and the Community in May 1997. This states, broadly, that schools should value the self, should value relationships, should value society and should value the environment.

The school curriculum should provide opportunities for all pupils to learn and achieve.

Inherent in this is the concept of inclusion - the idea that all pupils should have access to a broad and balanced curriculum. Inclusion means that all

pupils should be set challenges that are appropriate to their individual level of response. Different pupils have different needs, and bring into school different experiences, interests and strengths. The school curriculum should include ways to overcome any potential barriers to learning which pupils might have, specifically barriers created by a pupil's special educational needs, by a disability or by a pupil learning English as an additional language. The school curriculum should make clear how this philosophy of inclusion is going to be brought about in practice.

How your child's individual school manages this whole curriculum of learning will be described in the school prospectus and should be clear when you discuss the aims and values of the school with the teachers, head teacher and governors.

The school experience is about more than learning academic subjects. The school will be able to describe how it does this, and how it meets the requirements of the national curriculum.

However, it should also be able to describe clearly how it manages to meet philosophical, moral and social requirements, which is likely to be as important or indeed even more important to you as a parent. What

children learn at school is, after all, a great deal more than just how to read and count.

The National Curriculum

The National Curriculum grew out of the Education Act of 1996. It has four main stated purposes, which are to establish entitlement, to establish standards, to promote continuity and coherence and to promote public understanding.

The idea of entitlement is that all children have the same right to learning, regardless of any differences that they might have. These differences might include social background, culture, race, gender, abilities or disabilities. The national curriculum was designed to meet the needs of all pupils and as such, all pupils in maintained schools in England are entitled to follow it.

The expectations of learning and attainment are made explicit in the national curriculum, so that consistent standards can be established. These standards are national, and are the same regardless of where in England the child is being taught.

This shared entitlement to a single set of standards contributes to continuity, whether pupils remain in the same school or whether they move from school to school. It aims to give both continuity and coherence between different phases in a child's education, so that all schools at Secondary Level, for example, can rely on a shared experience of learning through KS1 and KS2.

Finally, the national curriculum is designed to promote understanding of what is learned in schools. Because all schools follow the same curriculum, books such as this one can be written, and all parents, teachers and pupils can have a shared understanding of 'what children learn in the classroom'.

****

CORE SUBJECTS

Chapter 2

Literacy

Literacy is divided into three components in the national curriculum:

1.Speaking and listening
2.Reading
3.Writing

Each has its own attainment targets, and each is examined separately in SATS tests. In reality, of course, the three strands are closely related. Speaking and Listening are how language is developed and communication skills honed. These skills are then enhanced by the ability to read what others (and what the child himself) have written, and writing is the ability to record this communication as effectively as possible in a permanent form.

Speaking and Listening

Much of Literacy is taught through Speaking and Listening, and this may be something that surprises parents. We are used to the teaching of reading and writing. Speaking, listening, responding, discussing, interacting and presenting are skills of which we may be less fully aware. A great deal of a child's learning in primary schools is done away from pencil, paper and computer. Children may sit in a group, perhaps on the floor, and learn through talking, sharing and doing. They will learn to listen to (and repeat) songs and rhymes, to listen to stories and poems. They will listen to instructions, to examples, to recounts of what they have learnt and done. They will learn to respond to these, to make comments, to use language to share what they know and think. They will need to learn to use language to communicate their ideas, to speak clearly and in sentences, to give a context to what they are saying, to repair when what they are saying is misunderstood. They need to develop the skill of asking the right question when they don't understand, and of framing that question in a way that will be understood.

Children will learn to recount events or stories, making their account sequential, with a beginning, a middle and an end. Gradually, they learn various techniques to make what they say more interesting. Is it more exciting if they hold back a secret until the end?

In a group, only one person can be heard at a time, so children need to learn to take turns. They will need, as well, to develop strategies for getting their turn heard (putting up a hand, for example.) They will need to learn to make their contribution relevant, and to listen out in case someone else makes their point first. They need to learn to both ask and to answer questions. They learn to act out scenes, both they themselves and by using toys as the characters.

They learn to give these characters voices, and to understand that when they are acting out a story in a group, they can only be the voice of one of these characters. They learn that when they are pretending, they are not being themselves.

As they get older, children learn to think about non-verbal techniques. Does it help if they stand up? Should they face their audience? Should they stand still? Would a hand gesture help make something clearer? What about language – are the words they are using the most effective for this talk? Does the audience understand what they are saying?

They learn that their language needs to alter depending on to whom they are speaking. This change in 'register' means that they should speak to the teacher in a different way from how they speak to their friends. When they are working in a group, how can they ensure that everyone understands?

When they are listening to a longer talk by an adult, children need to develop the technique of remembering the key points of what is said and putting these into their own words. They need to realise that they are not expected to remember everything, and that they can pick out the most important, or most interesting, parts of what they hear.

Finally, children need to learn to appreciate what many adults find difficult: that other people have different opinions or view to their own. They need to learn to acknowledge other people's views, and to make constructive criticisms of those views. They need to learn to accept criticism, and to manage it without heat. They need to learn that they are entitled to opinions, and should be able to defend those opinions calmly and clearly. They need to learn that others' opinions are equally to be respected.

Speaking and listening are the core skills of communication. Children will need to learn how to record what they think in written form, and to receive what others think through reading. Speaking and listening, however, are where communication begins. Through them children learn to manage language, to appreciate the power of words, to discuss, to dramatise, to negotiate, to recount and to present. A huge amount of their time at primary school will be spent on these skills, and just because there is little practical evidence produced of this work, its significance should not be underestimated.

How to help at home

It is, patently, daft to suggest that you speak to and listen to your child! We all of us as parents spend hours and hours listening to, encouraging, reprimanding, coaxing, haranguing, persuading and, let's face it, filtering out the chatter of our children. They are with us and part of our day-to-day, minute-to-minute world, and constant communication is part of that relationship.

On the other hand, plenty of adults spend time and money on learning how better to talk to, and listen to, a husband, wife or partner. This is because many of us find that, as time goes by in a relationship, our communication with each other can deteriorate. Perhaps, if we are honest, the same might be said of our communication with our children.

When they are very small, it takes considerable effort to communicate with our children. Babies cry, and we as parents have to work out why and find a way of putting whatever is wrong, right. Gradually the communication efforts of our infant become more sophisticated, although they remain unsubtle. A two-year-old who wants something may ask, and ask, and ask again until you respond. If we want to 'get through', we need to keep our language simple, perhaps squat down so our faces are of a level and focus on getting our message heard.

By the time our child starts school, and increasingly as she gets older, this communication becomes easier. Our child may burble through what has happened at school as we walk home. We take some of it in... and some of it we miss as we think through the contents of the fridge and try to work out what to have for dinner. As time goes on we may get to the point where, if we are not careful, we seldom *really* listen to our children, and they seldom really listen to us. By the age at which the advice in this book finishes, as the young person approaches puberty and the increased independence of secondary school, communication between parent and child can be pretty sporadic.

For us to help our child in speaking and listening skill development at school, we need to reverse this trend. We need to allow her to practice speaking across different contexts, and we need to give her opportunities to listen. In our busy lives this may sound artificial, but it is likely to have benefits right across our relationship with our child, so is well worth considering.

Try to put some time aside to really talk with your child. If you are really listening (and not just doing that thing that all parents do: nodding, saying "uhuh" and repeating the last thing back as a question if there's a pause!), then you will need to require her to really talk. If she has your undivided attention, it is reasonable to demand that she gives her full attention to what she is saying and how she says it. It encourages her to make what she is saying interesting, amusing or moving. By giving her an audience, you make far greater demands on the speaker.

You can also help her to become a better listener. Talk to her, really trying to make what you say interesting. You can also encouraging listening skills by reading aloud to her, or by listening to audio stories together (listening to stories together on long car journeys is great for this.)

You can also encourage an awareness of the skills of speaking and listening by going to things together. Take her to the theatre or to talks and events at your local library. If she is interested, enrol her in a drama course or sign up together for your annual village pantomime. If you attend church, synagogue, mosque or temple, encourage her to listen to what is said, and perhaps encourage her, as she becomes older, to get involved. Could she give a reading? Could she lead some prayers?

Speaking and listening are part of every day life, but that does not mean that they are easy, nor that we are all good at them. Like any skills, they get better with attention and with practice. Practising these skills with your child can be hugely rewarding, and have real and positive consequences for your ongoing relationship. It is well worth the effort.

Reading

Learning to read is one of the most amazing skills which children acquire. Through it, all the knowledge of the world becomes available. Without it, that knowledge is still there, but it is much harder to access.

Reading begins with picture books. Your son may bring home a reading book, which has no words. The idea is that you look at the pictures together, and that your son learns that the story unfolds sequentially, that it has a beginning, a middle and an end. The book-without-words is also a good introduction to the characters who will appear in your school's reading scheme. The names of these characters are often the first words the child will learn to 'sight recognise'.

The next stage is when a single word is introduced, for example "Look!", and where a single phrase, and then sentence, is added to each page. These sentences usually have plenty of repetition, so that the child can see that the words that look the same, sound the same. This is a huge first step in reading.

Of course, reading is more than memorising what words look like and being able to recognise them when they are seen. These 'sight words' are important, but so is the ability to 'decode' new words, and in order to do this, the child has to learn what the sounds of the word are. This 'phonetic' (sound-based) decoding begins with knowing the individual sounds of the letters of the alphabet.

You may have already taught your son his ABCs, possible through song. The trouble is that the ABC of the song does not give the phonetic sound of the letters. You will have to learn now to call them 'a' (as in the middle sound of 'cat') and 'b' as in the first sound in 'bat'. With the phonetic alphabet, your son can begin to 'sound out' unfamiliar words.

Initially, these words will be simple CVC (consonant, vowel, consonant) words such as 'hat', 'pot', 'let', 'sit' and so on. Gradually, this is expanded to include CCVC words such as 'stop', 'clip' and 'snap' and CVCC words such as 'hint', 'list' and 'best'. Using this technique, many longer words can be 'sounded out' and read.

However, English is not a phonetic language! Letters put together often make new sounds (like 'ch', 'sh', 'th' and so on), and these need to be learnt too. Sounds, that in English may be represented by more than one letter, may be called 'phonemes' in school. Just as the same sound (phoneme) in English can be made by different letters ('bluff' and 'enough'), so can different letters make different sounds ('hat' and 'hate', 'girl' and 'germ'). The same sounding word can look different ('bean' and 'been'), letters can be silent ('knight'), the same word can change how it is said according to context ('read' present tense and 'read' past tense)... the list is endless. English is a complicated language, and no one technique is going to work to master the reading of it. Children need to learn the rules of phonetics, to learn to 'sight read' common words, to use context, and to make educated guesses. The reading programme chosen by the school should steer them through this labyrinth in an ordered way.

Most schools have a system where the child brings home a reading book from the scheme each evening. Your job as parents is to listen to your child reading that book. The next book may not seem to you to follow on logically from the last (perhaps your child was on book 3b, and is now on book 2c), but this is probably because different strands of a scheme will give greater practice at different aspects of reading. What is important is that your child enjoys the reading and feels confident in what he is doing.

Gradually, reading becomes less a discreet activity, and more part and parcel of daily life in school. Your son may still bring a reading book home, but he is also reading a worksheet on Romans for history and the labels of the parts of the plant for science. He will also, increasingly, be reading back what he has written himself.

You may be asked to sign a reading diary each day to say that you have heard your child read. This is an opportunity also to raise any concerns, or to identify particular areas of weakness. Teachers will hear all children read at various times, and other adults may come into school to help. It is a fact of logistics, however, that not every child can be heard every time, nor all children heard very often, so your role in hearing your child read every day is a vital one. You need to record that he is doing well, to say if you think he has moved on beyond this stage of book, or to point out that he is struggling.

As he moves up the school, it is likely your son will be encouraged to keep this reading diary for himself, probably now as a reading journal. In this journal he will be asked to record what he has read (both school books and at home), and to begin to make a critical response to the books. Did he enjoy the book? What was its style? Has he read anything else by that writer? Would he recommend the book and if so, to whom?

Your son's reading should continue to progress, even after he has 'learnt to read'. He should be able to read more varied, and more advanced text, with increasing fluency and, probably, with increasing speed. He may develop the skill of 'scanning' or 'speed reading' a text in order to extract the meaning. He needs to be aware of the layout of what he reads (does the author use titles? Is the information divided into paragraphs, with subheadings?) If the writing is fiction, is it first person or third person? How is the personality of the character portrayed by what he says and by what he does? Your son should begin to be selective in his reading, to have a favourite author or genre. He should be able to say why he likes (and doesn't like) certain books, and to be able to understand the worth of books, even those he would not choose to read. He may begin to realise how current literature has grown out of the writing of the past, and begin to appreciate the value of a literary heritage.

How to help at home

Of all the skills taught at primary school, reading is probably the one that allows most, and in many ways relies most, on parental involvement. There are all sorts of theories about the effects of reading to your child. It is a truism (but may nevertheless be true) that Reception teachers can spot which children have been read to as babies from the moment they enter the classroom. Reading to, and with your child, really does help with that child's learning.

Reading with your child requires that you sit together, that you focus on the same thing and that you share the same experience. Although your child will bring home a 'reading book' from school each day, don't let that stop you reading on with her in other contexts. You can read familiar books together, the text so well known that if you skip a bit, you are immediately corrected! You can pore over the pictures together, looking at all the details and trying to guess what each character feels, or what he might be saying in his head. You can also read books to your child which are too difficult for her to read for herself (at whatever age she is). For the four-year-old, this may mean reading complete fairy tales; for the ten-year-old, this may mean reading Lord of the Rings – the theory is the same. By reading aloud, you are encouraging listening skills, and you are providing the pleasure of a more advanced read, without the effort. You are encouraging your child to see reading as a pleasurable and a worthwhile activity, and are modelling the value of reading to your child. Incidentally, do not underestimate the importance of letting your child see you read. Curling up in the chair with a good book may not feel like good child-care, but in actual fact you are providing an excellent role model!

As far as the practicalities of learning to read are concerned, your biggest responsibility is to listen to the reading book every night. Make this a priority, and show how much you value your child's progress. Try not to rush your child or correct her, but let her 'have a go' at unfamiliar words, and always praise her efforts. If she sees how proud you are of this new skill of reading, she will be motivated to keep on trying. Don't underestimate how difficult learning to read is. Perhaps you could try to teach yourself to read Japanese (or any other language which uses an unfamiliar script) alongside. It is fairly sure that your daughter will master her reading before you do!

You need not confine reading to books. Encourage your daughter to spot and read text all around her. Ask her to read signs, notices, the labels on ketchup bottles, the names on the post that comes through your door. Make reading fun and worth the effort. Leave her a note, printed clearly, with the letters formed in the way she is being taught, telling her that a treat is hidden under the sofa. She will be well motivated to puzzle it out.

As she masters the skill of decoding the words, move your emphasis on to helping her to understand the text of what she has read. Can she tell you what happened in the story in her own words? Did she enjoy the story? Why or why not? What was the 'best bit'? What does she think happens after the end of the book?

Don't forget to continue to encourage her to read aloud. Even after she has mastered silent reading, this is still a skill that is worth developing. Can she 'do' the voices? How can she make the story sound really exciting? If you have a younger child, encouraging your older child to read to him can be a great way to help them both.

Visit your library. In this technological age, book libraries may be an underused resource. Help your child make choices about which books to take out. How should she choose? Has she read anything else by the same writer? What does the front cover tell her? What about the 'blurb' on the back? If she shows an interest in a subject, encourage her to take out non-fiction books on that subject. Perhaps you are going to get a rabbit. Take out and read all the rabbit books in the library together, and see if all the advice tallies.

As she gets older and more proficient, reading becomes a solitary activity. Make sure that it does not become a lonely one. Many parents encourage reading in bed before lights out. This is fine, as long as the association does not become a negative one (being packed off to bed because the parents have had enough!). Perhaps you could allow reading time downstairs before bed instead. Perhaps this could be an opportunity for you to sit down quietly and read for half an hour yourself. Few of us have spaces like this in our busy lives, and perhaps helping your child could give you the excuse you need.

Of course, reading is more than just books. A child who is reading the instruction manual for a computer game is still reading. Send your daughter an e-mail – she will have to read it. You can also encourage wider appreciation of reading by, for example, watching the film-of-a-book together. How were the characters different? Was that how she had imagined the main character would look? Who would she have cast as the heroine?

Writing

Writing starts with pencil control. Your child may spend some considerable time joining dots, colouring and tracing lines in order to develop pencil control. He will also need to learn how to hold a pencil correctly, and how to position the paper. He will need to learn that writing in English progresses from top to bottom of the page, and from left to right.

The next stage is to learn to form letters. It is very important that you as parent become aware of how these letters are formed as they vary a little from style to style. (For example, does your son's school favour the looped top to the lower-case letter 'k', or prefer him to remove the pencil from the paper and to start with a new stroke?). Incidentally, the correct way of forming numbers is just as important, and you should check how he is being taught to do this as well. (Is he forming the number 8 by drawing an 's' and continuing round, or by drawing the 's' backwards?) Correct forming of the letters now will help greatly later, particularly when your son moves on to 'joined-up' writing further up the school.

Once he can form the letters, your son will be encouraged to put the 'sounds' together to make up words. If he can sound out 'c – a – t', he can write it down letter-by-letter, and so write the word.

Progression from this point varies. Sometimes your son may be encouraged to string sounds together and to write letters as they sound to him. Although this may not look like writing, it is an important step and is to be encouraged. If your son feels that by recording sounds in this way he is 'writing', this is a great step in building confidence. 'Emergent' writing of this type should be encouraged and not too much emphasis made on correcting it. Get your son to read what he has written back to you. If he were to make some breaks in the writing, would this make it easier to read back? Children are encouraged to put a 'finger space' (a space the size of their index finger) between words, and need repeated reminders to do this.

Emergent writing is a great way to encourage fluency, but children also need to learn accuracy. Often this is encouraged by the child copying a sentence, possibly from the white board or perhaps written in their books. They may be encouraged to tell the teacher what they want to write, and then to copy under that phrase when the teacher has written it. Another technique is to trace over the words written by the teacher.

Often all techniques will be used in the same piece of writing. Perhaps all the children in the class copy a first sentence from the board. Then they tell an adult what they want to write next and copy or trace over that sentence. Finally they may be encouraged to write another sentence by themselves. They may be encouraged to 'have a go' at unfamiliar words, sounding them out phonetically. As their reading becomes more fluent, so should their writing reflect this. 'Sight recognition' reading words may be the first words which are 'learnt' as spellings.

Just as reading can be taught as phonetics, each sound being termed a 'phoneme', so can writing be a reflection of this. If a sound is a phoneme, the written representation of a sound is a 'grapheme'. The phoneme 'a' (as in 'play') may be written by the graphemes 'ay' ('play'), 'ai ('tail'), 'a-e' ('late') or 'ey' ('prey'). The grapheme 'c' may be used to represent different phonemes ('cut', 'cease'). Children need to learn first which grapheme can be used to represent which phoneme, and then, later, the different graphemes which might be used, and which is correct. Some of this is done by learning rules, some by learning patterns, some by learning how to spell individual words.

Writing progresses in both fluency and accuracy. Children are encouraged to write independently to convey meaning, and to do so across a variety of different tasks. They may write a diary entry, label parts of the body, write speech bubbles to complete a cartoon, write a story, report an event. Along with their increased fluency, they are encouraged to improve accuracy. Finger spaces between words continue to be reinforced. They are encouraged to begin a sentence with a capital letter, and to end with a full stop. One or two spelling errors may be pointed out and corrected in each piece of writing.

Gradually children come to understand that what they write must be read by others, and not just be understandable to themselves.

Gradually, the effect of what they write is considered. How can they make their writing more interesting? More persuasive? More exciting? They are encouraged to vary sentence length, to consider which words to use, to employ adjectives and adverbs effectively. They are taught to vary punctuation, so that it includes commas, question marks, exclamation marks, speech marks, apostrophes and brackets. They are encouraged to use different writing techniques depending on the nature of that writing. A letter of complaint to the manager of a restaurant does not use the same language as a note to a friend. An exciting adventure story uses different techniques from a scientific report.

Children are encouraged to write clearly and legibly, and to use a variety of tools to help them to present their work accurately and effectively. They may use dictionaries to check both meaning and spelling of words, a thesaurus to widen vocabulary, a word-processing package to help with the presentation, a spell-checker to correct spelling and grammar. They learn to use language differently when speaking, writing, texting, e mailing or blogging, and to take conscious control of the different styles. Writing becomes a tool for communication across the whole curriculum, as well as an asset in daily life.

How to help at home

Although many children will have learnt to write their own name before they start school, in many ways you can be most helpful by not encouraging your child to write until she starts to learn formally. This is because different people have different ways of forming letters, and it can be very confusing to a child to have to re-learn a letter shape. One of the most important aspects of writing each letter is learning where to start. Children need to be taught where to put the pencil (At the top? In the middle?) and in which direction to move it (straight down? In a circle anti-clockwise?) Once your child has been taught how to do this at school, you can then be a great help in practising and reinforcing it. Making sure you are clear about how she is being taught can prevent problems later on.

Once you are in agreement about what each letter looks like, and how it is formed, you can help by reinforcing this knowledge. Help your child to write the letters, and say the letter sounds, in a variety of contexts. Write in the condensation of the bathroom window, draw letter shapes in flour when you bake, trace the shape in the sand of the sandpit. You can line up peas to form a letter on her plate, play a game where you try to guess the letter traced out on the palm of her hand, try to make the shapes of the letters with your bodies. Lots of short, fun activities across a variety of contexts are likely to help hugely. Not all children learn by making pencil marks on paper, and you have many opportunities throughout your day to take letter forming out into the wider world.

That said, you may find that your child wants to 'write'. If so, encourage her and don't worry too much whether what she writes makes any sense to you. The fact that she understands that marks on the paper represents sounds and words is a good first step, and the fact that she is enthusiastic about 'writing', and confident about it, is all to the good.

As her writing becomes more legible and more accurate, give her lots of real life opportunities to write. Ask her to write the shopping list for you, get her to write her Grandmother's name on the envelope when she sends her a picture, ask her to make a memo to stick to the front door saying 'keys!'

As well as encouraging emerging handwriting, you are in a good position to encourage typing skills. Few of us now use handwriting for anything other than our own use. We may jot ourselves a note or scribble a reminder, but if we are writing formally, we use a keyboard. We type our e-mails, and we word-process our letters. We seldom do more than sign our name using handwriting.

There are many computer games designed to familiarise children with the keyboard, and you are likely to have more time than is available at school to encourage their use. Let your son pick out the letters to send an e-mail. Let him scan in a favourite drawing and use the keyboard to add a title. Let him use your mobile phone to send a text message. The more he comes to realise that the ability to write is the power to communicate, the more he is likely to be motivated to learn.

You can encourage him, also, by 'scribing' for him. Let him dictate what he wants to say in an e-mail, and let him see the words appearing on the screen. He is still writing, even if you are physically entering the words. Writing is about the whole business of putting thoughts and ideas down on paper (or on the screen), and is about a great deal more than just the action of recording the marks. As his writing becomes more sophisticated, give him opportunities to use it to good end. Look for short story, news article or poetry competitions for children in magazines or in your local library, and encourage him to enter. Even if he does not win a prize in the actual competition, value his work. Pin it up on the kitchen board, or put it in a folder for him to keep.

There is a lot to be said for showing how proud you are of his progress!

Writing is also, of course, a great way to keep in touch. Encourage your child to write a letter to a friend who has moved away, a postcard from on holiday to his grandmother, a birthday card to his uncle. It can be a great motivation to encourage letter writing before birthdays, Christmas or other festivals, especially if the child has a present he particularly wants! He could write a letter of request to Santa, or to his Aunt in Australia. Either way, he will be using his writing to communicate in a way that makes a great deal of sense to him.

****

Chapter 3

Numeracy

Numeracy, as taught through the National Curriculum at primary school, can be broken down into four sections:

1.Using and applying mathematics
2.Number and algebra
3.Shape, space and measure
4.Handling data.

Using and applying maths

The first of these is rather odd, in that it is really about how the others are used. Children should be using their numeracy throughout their lives, as an integral part of most classroom activities. The ability to use and apply maths will depend on the understanding of that maths as taught in the other sections.

Throughout their time at school (and, it is hoped, in life) children learn to tackle real-life problems requiring mathematical approaches. They are encouraged to picture the problem, and to work out what they need to do to work out the answer. What are they being asked? What, actually, is the question?

They are then encouraged to use what they know of numeracy to tackle the problem. Will they need to calculate or to estimate? Are they being asked to add, subtract, multiply or divide? Do they need to bring to bear their understanding of measure? Of time, space or shape? Is there a formula they could use which would help in this situation? Do they need to gather their data together into a more cohesive form? Do they have all the data they need?

When they have identified which part of their numeracy knowledge is best suited to solving the problem, children need to apply what they know of solving that problem. Which techniques should they use? Should they use a mental maths approach, informal jottings, a written method, a calculator? How many steps will be needed to work out the solution to this problem? Are the same techniques needed for each stage, or would different ones work better at different points?

When they have done their calculations, they need to check back. Does the answer make sense? Does it, in fact, solve the problem with which they were faced? Do they have an answer?

In order to have the techniques available to them to answer real-life problems, children need to be competent at all aspects of numeracy. The first of these is their use of number.

Number and algebra

Number and algebra is what most of us think of as 'Maths'. It is about counting, about adding and subtracting, about multiplying and dividing.

However, before children can begin to work with numbers they need to learn those numbers, learn their names, their order and to learn what those numbers look like. In other words, children need to learn to count.

This learning to count takes place in school all the time (and probably has started before that) through number songs, number books and number games. Children learn to 'recite' their numbers, but they still need to learn that each number corresponds to an amount. They are helped in this by constant and repeated counting throughout their day – how many books am I holding up? How many chairs are there around the craft table? How many bottles are left on the tray?

This repeated counting is done practically, also, with real, small objects. With these, children are encouraged to physically move the objects across as they say the number, so that for example, as they count beads on a string they push them to the other end one by one, saying "1, 2, 3" etc. They learn that when you do this, the last number that you say is the amount of objects. Gradually, this awareness of number is expanded to include recognising written numbers.

Children count sequentially following the numbers on a number track. They are asked then to identify the numbers without reciting from the beginning (for example, 'can you point to the number 3?')

A number track is simply a set of numbers, presented horizontally, running from 0 to 10. It is important that it starts with the number '0', as the children need to learn that '0' is a number, even though they may have used it seldom when reciting their numbers. They learn that '0' is the number that means 'none.'

The next thing which children need to learn may again, like the last number when counting being the amount, seem obvious to us as adults. This is that once a set of numbers has been counted, we know how many are there – and that number stays the same *even if the objects are moved around into different position.*

Some children find this a difficult concept to grasp, and it may need constant and repeated reinforcement. If you have counted 7 buttons onto the plate, there are still 7 there, whether you line them up, place them in a circle or spread them out randomly.

It is essential that this constancy is fully grasped before the child is ready to even begin to think about addition or subtraction.

Addition

The next massive step, once the child can count how many objects are there, is to begin to understand when that number changes. When the number of objects is increasing, this is the beginning of addition.

Pupils are taught that it is possible to 'count' objects by correspondence to other objects. Therefore, if we have 3 cups and we put one cup each onto a saucer, we know we have 3 saucers. Equally, but more difficult, if we have 3 cups and put one cup each onto a saucer yet have 2 saucers left over, then we know that there are 2 more saucers than there are cups, and 2 more than 3 is 5.

The next technique for addition is to put a first number into the child's head (children often do this by physically tapping the forehead and saying the number) and then counting on from that number using fingers. Therefore 3 is held in the head, and the child counts on two more finger ("4, 5") and so arrives at the correct number.

Slightly different is the concept that addition is the act of combining two numbers. Children may count out 3 beads on a tray, and then count out 2 beads on the tray…and then be asked to count all the beads. This technique is useful to teach the concept that addition is finding a total, and therefore it doesn't matter which set of beads is counted first. Most of the work at this stage will be done orally, with an emphasis on the ideas making sense.

There is frequent use of 'number sentences' – saying the addition facts out loud. In the examples above, whichever technique had been used, the children would be encouraged to realise, and to say, that 'Three and two are five'. This sentence might be written up on the white board. Gradually, there is a move towards writing these as $3 + 2 = 5$ (in other words, using mathematical symbols to replace the words), but they are still spoken and are still number sentences. They are written horizontally, so that they can be read, spoken and (it is hoped) understood. The vocabulary used for these number sentences is varied – involving 'altogether make', 'is more than', 'is greater than' and 'is the same as' as well as, finally, 'plus' and 'equals'.

The idea that addition can be done in any order continues to be reinforced as children become more confident, and gradually they are encouraged to realise that putting the larger number first and 'adding on' a smaller one is far easier. Twelve and two more is a great deal easier to work out than two, and twelve more!

They are encouraged also to look for patterns, such as pairs of numbers which make ten (often called 'number bonds to ten'), or numbers which are doubles. By adding these known facts up first, sums can be made simpler. $7 + 6$ (which equals 13) $+ 3$ is clumsy, whereas if you know that 7 and 3 make ten, it is easy then to add on the 6.

In the same way, 7 + 2 makes 9, and then adding another 7 is more difficult than knowing that two 7s are 14, and then adding on the 2.

$$7 + 2 + 7 =$$

$$14 + 2 = 16$$

Similarly, children come to understand that adding 9 or 11 is easier if they add 10 and then adjust up or down by one. At this stage they may learn to 'partition' larger numbers into tens and units, and add them in their component parts. The numbers can then be recombined.

$$83 + 14 =$$

$$90 + 7 = 97$$

This can be expanded to work with even larger numbers.

$$244 + 135 =$$

$$300 + 70 + 9 = 379$$

The emphasis on 'working out' number problems continues throughout primary education. This 'mental maths' forms a large part of the children's learning, and is even examined separately in the SATS exams. As numbers become too big for them to hold in their heads, they are encouraged to use informal jottings to remember them, and this progresses gradually to more formal recording methods.

One of the most important concepts for this more formal writing is that of place value. It is essential that children understand that a large number may have hundreds, tens and units, and that if there are, for example, no tens, a '0' must be used to 'hold the place'. To help with this, they may initially use a grid, labelled H, T and U.

	H	T	U
Three hundred and forty two:	3	4	2
Five hundred and six:	5	0	6

Gradually, as children become more confident, the grid is dropped...

```
358 +
 73
 11
120
300
431
```

...and eventually the process is contracted and they move onto the standard 'carrying' method, remembered from our youth.

```
358 +
 73
431
 1 1
```

Subtraction

The concept of subtraction, like addition, comes out of counting. The children are encouraged to 'find one less than' a given number, and then '2 less' and so on. It may be more difficult to do this than to find 'more than', since the numbers are not so familiar recited backwards (and, indeed, considerable time is now given in schools to practising 'counting backwards' as a skill.)

In the same way that addition was taught by the concept of 'how many altogether?', so subtraction may be taught with the concept of 'how many are left?'

7 beads are placed on a tray, then 2 are taken away. The children count how many beads are left and so work out the answer.

In this way children are encouraged to find out *difference*. They work, as before, with real situations and in sentences. They may be encouraged to count the beads on the tray (9), and then to look away while some are removed. They then count the remaining beads (4). How can they tell how many have been taken away? The answer is to find out the difference. They count from 4 (the amount that are there) up to 9 (the amount there were there), or from 9 (the amount there were) down to 4 (the amount there are now). Either way, this takes five hops on the number track, or five fingers... so the answer must be 5.

Although subtraction may seem more difficult than addition, it is likely the two will be taught simultaneously. The relationship between the two is important to grasp – and useful. If children can understand that 7 and 3 together make 10, they can be helped to grasp that 10 – 3 must be 7 (and that 10 – 7 = 3!)

The number line (the more 'grown up' version of the number track) can be a huge help with working out subtraction facts. The child finds, for example, the smaller number and uses the number line to hop up to the larger.

The amount 'hopped' is the 'difference', and therefore the subtraction answer.

E.g. $7 - 3 = 4$

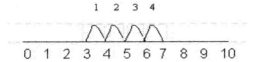

Using the same number line the same sum may be reinforced by starting at the larger number, the 7 and hopping down the track to the 3. This still takes 4 jumps, so the answer is 4. This duplication of the same sum using different techniques is used to reinforce understanding. Children are taught to find "ways to work it out" rather than merely being given one method. This understanding that there may be more than one way to arrive at the answer – but that the answer remains the same – all helps to facilitate better understanding in the child.

As they get more advanced, the line becomes blank and is used merely as a visual prompt. This is often called 'bridging'. Children are taught to count up (or down) to the nearest 10, and then make hops in 10s until they finish again in units.   Therefore, $16 - 7 =$ is seen as the difference between 16 and 7, and that difference counted.

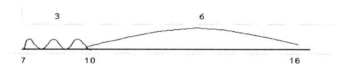

$3 + 6 = 9$ (So $16 - 7 = 9$)

The children's understanding of the relationship between subtraction and addition means that they can use one to check the other. Therefore, if they have worked out that 17 − 4 = 13 they can check this by working out whether 13 + 4 really does equal 17.

The empty number line method of recording their thoughts is used throughout primary school (…and, now I've learnt it I've been known to use it myself!). During Mental Maths sessions it is an excellent way to record the child's thinking.

As with addition, the children need to be confident about place value before setting out sums vertically. As before, they need to be reminded to use '0' as a place-holder. They learn that 467-203 = is the same as

467 -
203
———

In other words, they learn to turn the number line vertically and partition at the same time. This allows the more formal method of subtracting in columns. They will need to be reminded that they have to start the subtraction, just like in addition, with the units.

In the sum above, there is no problem with doing the subtraction in columns.

467 -
203
264

However, things become more difficult when some of the numbers in the columns cannot be subtracted from each other, as the one in the top line is smaller than that in the bottom.

E.g.

502 -
356
———

There are two commonly used methods to deal with this. One is subtraction by equal addition (where you change the bottom number as you go along.) The other is subtraction by decomposition (where you change the top number as you go along.) As a HUGE generalisation, most of us – parents – will have been taught the former, and most children will now be taught the latter – although probably not until Year Seven.

It doesn't matter which they learn (both work), but if your child is learning one method you could do untold damage by trying to show her the other. My advice is to wait and see which she is taught at secondary school, and then get her to show you how to do it!

<u>Multiplication</u>
Multiplication begins with 'learning doubles'. As with number-bonds to 10, these are useful facts to learn. Children may also learn to count in 10s – but there is unlikely to be much formal multiplication work until the children become really confident with number recognition and number order.

When they do start multiplication work, it tends to come out of addition, and to be seen as repeated addition. Therefore, three lots of five are 5 + 5 + 5. Often this is represented visually in what are termed 'arrays', so that the concept of what is being asked can be fully understood.

i.e Two sets of dots in fours horizontally show 2 x 4

…and four sets of dots paired vertically show 4 x 2

...but each uses 8 dots.

Most of multiplication remains very visual at this age. Children are encouraged to group numbers (e.g. 'Ring these twelve sheep into groups of 3 - four groups of three make twelve'.) Only when the children are really clear about what multiplication (lots of the same number) really is, do they start to rote-learn their multiplication facts (what we used to call 'tables').

Multiples are (let's face it!), dull – but they are phenomenally useful as the child progresses with maths. Children can be encouraged in the harder multiples by it being explained that multiplication can be done in any order, so that many of the number facts can be 'done the easy way'. A child who does not know her 8 times multiple facts, but does know her 2 times multiple facts, may not know what 2 x 8 =, but does know that 8 x 2 + 16!

Formal multiplication begins, again, with the number line. Children make jumps along the line in hops of the same number e.g.

3 x 3 =

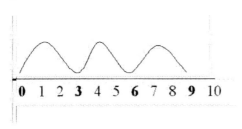

Next, the children begin to use the 'grid' method. This involves breaking the number down into its component parts – in other words, units, tens, hundreds… and so on. Incidentally, many adults say that to multiply by ten, 'add a zero' (e.g. 10 x 2 = 2 with an added '0' …20) This can lead to considerable confusion, so instead children are encouraged now to see that multiplying by ten moves the number a place to the left.

e.g.

2 x 10 =

Hundreds	Tens	Units
		2
	2	0

2 x 10 = 20

Initially, when using a grid, only one number will be greater than units. However, it works up until both numbers may involve units and tens, and hundreds and - ultimately thousands, tens of thousands, millions...

So, to summarise: '3 x 5 = ' is worked out using known multiple facts – or by repeated addition: 3 + 3 + 3 + 3 + 3, possibly using a number line.

'3 x 15 =' is worked out by breaking 15 into tens and units...

   3 x 10 = 30
   3 x 5 = 15

...and the two are added together: 30 + 15 = 45

'32 x 15 =' is worked out by separating ('partitioning') both the 32 (3 tens and 2 units) and the 15 (1 ten and 5 units)

e.g.32 x 15

X	30	2	
10	300	20	300 + 20 = 320
5	150	10	150 + 10 = 160

320 + 160 = 480

Gradually this is written without the grid, although children are still encouraged to write the workings beside each calculation in order to show the progression…

$$
\begin{array}{r}
250 \times \\
13 \\
\hline
2500 \\
750 \\
\hline
{\scriptstyle 1} \\
3250 \\
{\scriptstyle 1}
\end{array}
$$

Until ultimately they can do it without the notation, using the standard method.

Division

The understanding of division begins with simple sharing activities, or with the children being asked to group objects. For example, there are 6 shoes. How many pairs is that? Each table may be given 4 pencils. How many pencils will each child get if there are 2 children at each table? How many pencils would they need if they each want 3 pencils?

The concept of division is introduced as that of 'sharing or grouping *equally*. If there are 9 biscuits, and 3 children – how can the biscuits be shared out equally? If they are to be put into equal groups, how many would be in each group?

(This concept of 'fairness' is very dear to children, and makes division a matter of practical interest!)

As before, practical examples are written as number sentences, gradually introducing the symbol $(\div)$

"If 9 biscuits are shared out equally between 3 children, they will each get 3 biscuits"

...becomes:
"9 shared between 3 is 3"
...and is then written as:
"$9 \div 3 = 3$"

Another method is to explain that, just as multiplication is repeated addition, so division is repeated subtraction.
So, for example, if there are 15 sheep in a field, and the shepherd takes away five sheep, how many are left? How many are left if he takes 5 more? How many groups of 5 were there? How many 5s make 15? $15 \div 5 = 3$.

Since multiplication is the opposite (or inverse) of division, multiplication can be used to check division facts. Therefore, if $15 \div 5 = 3$, then $5 \times 3 = 15$ and $3 \times 5 = 15$ and, even, $15 \div 3 = 5$. This is sometimes referred to in school as 'buy one, get three free', in the manner of the supermarket special offer. Just like the special offer, it is an attractive concept to the children! While we are looking at sheep, there is a useful distinction to be made here.

Children, when exploring the early stages of division, are encouraged to both share numbers and to group numbers.

So they might be asked to ring the 12 sheep in the field discussed in the multiplication section, putting them into groups of 3. They would then count the groups and understand that four lots of three make twelve, and that 12 divided into 3s gives 4 groups. Similarly – but different – they might be asked to share the 12 sheep equally amongst 4 pens. Twelve sheep shared between four pens gives three sheep per pen.

Gradually, the children come to a point where they need to write down, or record their thoughts. As before, this is encouraged initially in an informal way, perhaps using hand-held whiteboards rather than paper to make it clear these are rough, temporary jottings to help 'working out', and are a long way from the formal written methods used traditionally.

Just as subtraction was easier using addition, so division is easier using multiplication. Children are encouraged to find division facts by 'hopping on' along a number line.

$25 \div 5 =$ is worked out by counting the number of hops of 5 along the number line.

See overleaf.

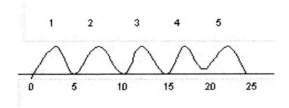

The next step is to use a more formal method (Chunking!)

Initially this still involves grouping the numbers. So $60 \div 5$ = might be worded as 'How many groups of 5 are there in 60?' To work this out the children would calculate that there are 10 lots of 5 in 50, and 2 lots of 5 in the remaining 10. 10 plus 2 equals 12.

$$60 -$$
$$\underline{50} \ (10 \times 5)$$
$$10 -$$
$$\underline{10} \ (2 \times 5)$$
$$0$$

$$10 + 2 = 12$$

Anything 'left over' is recorded as a 'remainder'.

Therefore, $87 \div 2$ can be worked out as follows: (overleaf).

```
87 -
80 (40 x 2)
 7 -
 6 (3 x 2)
 1
```

40 + 3 = 43 remainder 1.

This same method can be written in a more formal style.

i.e.

```
      43 r 1
2 ) 87
    80 (40 x 2)
     7
     6 (3 x 2)
     1
```

Gradually children learn to do this without the "chunks" on the side, and to move towards the standard written method.

They will learn (probably in secondary school) to treat division numbers digit by digit – but the chunking method should have helped understanding of what they are doing, rather than a mere following of a formula.

Shapes and measures
Shapes and measures starts off with basic positional language, and with using and understanding concepts such

as 'bigger' and 'smaller'. Children learn the names of the basic shapes, including circle, square, triangle and rectangle, and learn what it is that makes those shapes (for example, how many sides does it have? How many corners?) Children are also introduced to the concept of time, particularly with relation to the sequence of events. Language such as "First we draw the outline, and then we colour it in" moves towards the terms first, second, third and so on.

Gradually, children move onto recognising 3-dimensional shapes. They learn that a circle (2-dimensional) correlates to a sphere in 3 dimensions. They learn about cubes, prisms and pyramids, and learn to count the vertices (corners) and edges to describe the properties of shapes. They learn about rotating, or turning objects, and about symmetry, and they learn to describe how an object has been moved, and to compare one object with another. They learn to estimate, measure and weigh objects to better be able to describe them, and to make accurate comparisons one with another.

They learn the four compass directions, and to use them to describe the position of objects on a grid. They learn about turns and angles, and that a right angle is a turn of 45 degrees. They learn about time by learning the order of the days of the week and the months of the year, and by understanding that time is measured in units. They learn to recognise hours, then half-hours and quarters (on an analogue clock), and that hours are divided into minutes, and minutes into seconds.

They learn appropriate measures for time, distance and weight (you wouldn't calculate the reign of Queen Victoria in seconds, nor try to weigh a grain of salt using kilograms.)

As they progress to Key Stage 2 children begin to be able to understand about time as a concept, and to begin to estimate and to appreciate time. They learn to tell the time, using both digital and analogue formats, and to calculate the length of time that has passed given start and end times. Gradually they learn am and pm, and to read a 24 hour clock. They learn to read timetables and calendars, and are able to predict an end time, given a duration.

They learn about area and perimeters in shapes, and to use formula to work these out. They learn about volume and surface area, about measuring, estimating and calculating, about fractions and decimals. By the time they move to secondary school, children have been given a working knowledge of the whole 'business' which is mathematics.

Data
The final strand of numeracy is to do with handling data. Initially, this is simple recording of what they have learnt, and may be as simple as all the children with blue socks standing in one part of the room, those with grey in another and those with another colour in a third. This moves towards similar sorting of small objects (all the green counters together, all the blue counters together and so on), and from there to drawing the counters in the correct place

on a diagram. Different diagrams are introduced, and their uses discussed. How would it be best to record which is the most popular colour of sock?

Gradually the questions become more complex. Children are encouraged to collect data, and to record it using a variety of lists and tables, including block graphs, tick charts (frequency tables), pictograms, line graphs, bar charts, pie charts, carol diagrams, venn diagrams and so on. They may use ICT to enhance their data gathering and interpreting. They are encouraged to gather material accurately, to present it clearly and to use it to draw conclusions. They learn, also, to read data and to use what they read in solving problems. They are taught to use data to record, to solve, and to identify further questions to ask. Are they collecting the right data to answer the question? Are they presenting it in the most efficient way?

How to help at home with numeracy

Parents are often a huge help, particularly in the early stages of numeracy. Singing counting sings with your child (10 green bottles, 5 little ducks etc) is a great way to help get the sequence of numbers really familiar. Use opportunities for counting all the time, from when your baby is really small. Count the buttons as you do them up; count the toys back into the toy box; check all five soft toys are ready for bed. The simple sequence of numbers can be a great way to get early interaction with a young child, and all helps with number familiarity.

What may be more difficult to remember is to expand this as the child gets a little older. You can use exactly the same process with a slightly older child, but counting in 2s, finding doubles, sorting numbers into odds and evens, counting up in tens or counting backwards from one hundred for Hide and Seek. Numbers are all around, and can be a great resource for playing games. 'Collect' numbers as you walk to school – who can be the first to spot a number 7? Who will be the first to find two numbers that add up to 10? Who can start with 10 and by 'losing' the numbers seen be the first to get down to zero? Parents often forget the 'counting back' part of learning numbers. Many is the parent who counts the stairs on the way up – but how many remember to count back down again (backwards) on the way down?

Some of the more formal learning done in school can also be supported at home. Children need to learn various number facts: number bonds to ten ($9 + 1 = 10$, $8 + 2 = 10$, $7 + 3 = 10$ etc), number bonds to one hundred ($90 + 10 = 100$, $80 + 20 = 100$ etc), doubles ($1 + 1 = 2$, $2 + 2 = 4$, $3 + 3 = 6$ etc), multiples ($1 \times 2 = 2$, $2 \times 2 = 4$, $3 \times 2 = 6$ etc). Many of these are, frankly, quite dull to learn, but are extremely useful to know. You can provide the motivation by, for example, having a 'multiples' chart with various rewards and motivators when each has been mastered. Follow the school's lead and make sure that the challenges you are setting are in line with what is being taught at school.

Perhaps the best way that parents can help with numeracy is to provide opportunities to use number, away from official learning time. If you are cooking with your child, choose a recipe designed for four people and make it for only two. Your child can work out the halves of all the ingredients. If the cooking time is 35 minutes, your child can work out when the cake needs to be taken out of the oven. If you are shopping, you could give your child the change from the five pound note if he can tell you what it will be after you have bought bread (£1.38), sausages (£2.49) and a tin of baked beans (67p)!

In fact, the two chief areas where parents can provide learning opportunities more effectively than the school are those of time and money. I have even heard it said that, if you want to help your child with maths, buy her a watch!

If your child has an analogue watch with a good, clear face and numbers, there will be countless opportunities throughout the day for her to learn and use the concept of time. Ask her what time it is. Tell her she can play on the computer for ten more minutes, and then ask her what time that means she is going to stop. Warn her that dinner is 1.00pm and ask her how long you have to walk the dog. Ask her to set the DVD recorder. Digital time is all around and children will become familiar with it from mobile phones, in-car displays, computers etc. However, they need help to understand it, and to convert between analogue and digital, and to move to a 24-hour clock.

Look up timetables together. If you are going on holiday, work out together the times of the flights or the ships. How long is the journey? Does the destination country have their clocks set to the same time as ours?

Even more important to experience in the 'real world' (i.e. out of school) is money. Schools use plastic coins or pictures of coins – but it is all rather dry. Even in the 'real world', in an era where we all of us pay, more and more frequently, using 'plastic', children may be losing the opportunity which handling real money can bring. Quite difficult concepts such as units, tens and hundreds become simple when they are translated to money. A child is unlikely to get mixed up between a penny, a ten-pence piece and a pound coin, especially if the money is his own. The business of shopping, of buying an item and then working out how much change you should get, is probably the biggest use of numeracy in most of our lives. If you get £1.50 pocket money a week, how long is it going to take you to save up for the new Dr Who toy costing £4.99? How much money will you have left over that week when you finally buy it? These calculations (or ones very similar) are what we do all the time, whether we're deciding if we can afford to replace the cooker, considering changing our mortgage provider or working out a saving plan for a new extension.

Don't forget to let your child 'play' with the calculator. Calculators are fun (and pretty close to magic!) and they give children the opportunity to play with numbers, even very large numbers, without the feeling that they will get them wrong.

One whole paper in the SATS exams at KS2 uses calculators, so the more familiar children are with them, the better.

These sorts of 'applications of maths' are probably more useful than too much help with the numeracy done on paper at school. Once the child is working with formal written methods, these become quite abstract, and even slight differences in how sums are worked out can be confusing.

If you use the subtraction by equal addition method (making the number at the bottom larger) and your child is being taught subtraction by decomposition (making the number at the top smaller), the two methods can so easily become muddled, even if your child is just watching you work. You won't mean to, but you can undermine your child's confidence in the way he is working. Much better is to set the challenges, as mentioned above, and then watch how he works it out. If he gets the answer wrong, change the challenge to a slightly easier one, until he does get it right. Ask your child to explain his thinking and value his method, rather than stepping in and telling them your way. Reinforce what he does know, and give him plenty of real-life opportunities to practice using what he knows – this is far more use than trying to 'put right' what he is getting wrong.

Above all, your job is to his boost confidence and to help him to feel that he can use his knowledge and to work out problems. Tell him he is good at numeracy – such a view of himself can only be good!

****

Chapter 4

Science

Science is the other 'Core' subject of the national curriculum (along with Literacy and Numeracy). As such it is assessed as part of SATS at the end of Key Stages 1 and 2 (see chapter 7) It is divided into four sections:

1. Scientific enquiry
2. Life processes and living things (which loosely introduces Biology)
3. Materials and their properties (which loosely introduces Chemistry)
4. Physical processes (which loosely introduces Physics)

Scientific Enquiry

Children, from the very earliest age, learn about how the world around them works, and are taught about how a scientific enquiry into what they experience should take place. To begin with this is as simple as deciding what they want to find out, and explaining how they are going to do this. Gradually, they are introduced to the concept of a 'fair test' – fairness (as mentioned on page 62) being an important concept to most children. They are encouraged to ask questions, and to work out which question are the right questions to ask. If, for example, they are trying to work out what makes an object roll faster down a slope, what questions should they ask? Should the questions be about the colour of the objects, or the size of the objects or about their shape? They are encouraged to plan their investigations, and to come up with ways to answer the questions they have asked.

They are also encouraged to predict what the answer to the question is going to be before they put their investigation into practice, and to begin to formulate reasons as to why what happens, happens.

When doing experiments, the children are encouraged to use their senses, as appropriate, to record what they see, hear, smell, taste and touch, and are taught about basic safety rules in connection with these. Having recorded their results, they are taught how to analyse them and evaluate them. Did the experiment show what they wanted it to show? Was it a fair test? Finally, they are encouraged to present, communicate and share their results, and are encouraged to view the results of others' experiments. What have they learnt?

Life processes and living things
Children begin to take on board facts about a scientific subject. They learn, specifically, what makes a thing 'living', and although scientific enquiry is still encouraged, they need also to learn the facts about what a 'living thing' constitutes.

They learn the difference between what is living and what has never been alive, and that living things obey various principles (e.g. they move, feed, grow, use their senses and reproduce.) They learn the basics of classification, whether it be between 'alive' and 'not alive', or between 'plant' and 'animal', between 'carnivore', 'herbivore' or omnivore' or so on.

They study humans as animals, how we are the same as other animals and what is needed to keep us - and all animals - healthy. They learn about diet and exercise, about the senses and how they are used, about the life cycle from baby to old age. They learn about the difference between plants and animals, and about the parts of a plant and how it moves, feeds, grows, uses its senses and reproduces. They learn about how the environment around it affects a living thing and through this the basics of caring for the environment around themselves.

Materials and their Properties

Classification, as already begun through study of life processes and living things, continues as children look at materials. They learn to group materials according to their properties – in other words, to sort them according to similarities and differences. They may use any of their senses to decide on this sorting: materials may be hard or soft, salty or sweet, transparent or opaque, smelly or odourless, loud or quiet. Having sorted them, they look at what makes a material suitable for its job.

Which would be the best material for a pillow? For a window? For a nursery floor? Why?

As part of this understanding of materials, pupils look at how the materials can be changed, and at how permanent changes are. A sheet of rubber can be crumpled, but returns to its previous form. A sheet of paper, when crumpled, remains crumpled. Water when heated turns to steam, which when cooled returns to water. Ice when heated becomes water and when cooled returns to ice. An egg when heated (boiled) becomes cooked hard, and when cooled remains hard (a hard-boiled egg!) This exploration of materials and their properties encourages understanding of objects, natural and man-made, around them.

Physical Processes

Children are taught about forces and motion, about electricity, about light and sound.

They look at how objects move, what makes them move, what makes them speed up or slow down. They explore the forces of pushing and pulling, and how applying such forces will make an object move. They are taught about simple electric circuits, about how to build them and how to power them, and they look for the results of a successful circuit (for example, the bulb lights or the buzzer sounds.) They look at how a switch interrupts or completes the circuit. They identify light sources, whether those be natural (the sun) or man-made, and they learn that darkness is the absence of light. They learn that both sound and light travels in waves.

How to help at home with Science

Science can sound daunting to parents, and you may feel it is a subject best left to the experts – to the school, or perhaps to the makers of expensive science kits for home use.

In fact, although the kits can be fun, science at primary school level is more about looking at the world, asking why things happen, working out how things work, testing whether you are right. More than anything it is about problem solving, and as such you are well placed to give your child problems!

You could, for example, 'drop' a large amount of salt onto your dry rice granules. Too much salt, you could remind your child, may be bad for the heart. How can you separate the salt granules from the rice?

Your daughter may come up with several suggestions, some which may work better than others. She might suggest a fine sieve, since the salt granules are smaller than the rice. She might suggest soaking in water, since salt dissolves and rice does not. She might, even, suggest using static electricity created by rubbing a balloon on her jumper, because the salt grains are lighter than the rice. Whatever she suggests, let her have a go and discuss with her whether the suggestion works and why or why not.

She may be keen to get a pet, and you instead give her a pet rock, and swear blind that it is alive. How can she prove to you that it is not? If she does manage to prove this to your satisfaction, can she also tell you the needs that a hamster, for example, has in order for it to stay alive? How is she going to meet those needs?

You might give her the problem of designing a hot-water-bottle cover to give as a present for a relative's birthday. What material would be best to keep the bottle warm? How can she test if she is right? What other properties should the material have? Need it be soft? Need it be waterproof?

You could investigate, together, a torch that is not working. How can you tell what is wrong? Should you, perhaps, change one element at a time (first check the batteries, then the bulb, then check the connection inside)?

Science is about being prepared to 'have a go', and about understanding the safety requirements before you do so. It would not be a good idea for your child to 'have a go' at fixing a mains electricity device, for example, especially while it is still plugged in. With all experiments, though, after safety considerations have been addressed, it is important not to worry too much about mess or waste. If you never manage to separate the salt from the rice, you may have to throw them both away. If your child isn't able to risk getting it wrong, she will not be able to risk working it out for herself in the first place. Sometimes helping your child with her education is as much about gritting your teeth and putting up with a minor disaster zone as it is about formal teaching!

****

Chapter 5

Non-Core Foundation Subjects

The remaining subjects covered during your child's time at primary school are what are termed 'non-core'. However, this is a slightly misleading term, as most are compulsory during these years (those that are not are described as 'non-Statuary' and are described later). All of the non-core foundation subjects will all be covered at some time during Key Stages 1 and 2, and although they do not have as many hours devoted to them as do the core subjects, they remain an important introduction to each subject. Often they will be tackled all together as part of project work. A topic such as 'Changes' might cover the way the environment (geography), is changing due to developments in communication (ICT), how this effects what we hear and to what (and when) we listen (music), how it effects our activity levels (P.E) and the way in which our food is packaged (D and T)... as compared against 100 years ago (history). In this way, all the subjects will be covered, but the children may not always see them as separate lessons.

Design and technology
Design and technology is one of those subjects that make parents freeze in their tracks. What *is* it?

According to the National Curriculum, D & T is about looking at opportunities, needs and wants and developing ideas, products and systems which meet those opportunities, needs and wants. …which doesn't really make anything much clearer!

In D & T children are encouraged to look at a range of familiar products, work out how they work, decide why they have been designed that way and evaluate if, and why, they are successful. They are given tasks to design, using various products, and are encouraged to experiment, plan, develop their ideas, work together and – ultimately – build their products.

They should look at their own ideas critically, and also look at how other people have tackled similar problems recently, through history and in differing cultures. They should be able to discuss their ideas, and to be able to adapt them to be realistic within the confines of the materials available to them (a gold ring might be aesthetically pleasing, but a bent paperclip is more likely in school!) They should, though, be able to discuss ideal materials, tools, equipment and components and be able to come up with realistic alternatives. They will need to be able to draw what they want to do, discuss it, plan, measure, shape or cut materials as needed, assemble and attach different components and consider the appearance of their finished product.

Once they have built their product, they will need to show that they are able to evaluate it critically and both say why it works and what might be improved. If their product has failed to achieve what it set out to do, they should be able to make considered suggestions about what they might do differently another time.

How to help at home

Your children probably do this sort of thing all the time already, and you didn't realise that it was called Design and Technology! Every child who comes up with an ambitious plan for a new machine for sorting Lego, a design for a paper tower, a string-and-cardboard den, a new flavour of frozen smoothie lolly is, in fact, using his D & T skills. Your role is to let him (in spite of the mess!), to encourage (even when you know it won't work), to make suggestions without taking over (it's okay to suggest folding the paper to make it stronger, not so good to push him out of the way and do it yourself) and to deal with the disappointment when the project falls apart half way through.

Most children seem to love this building, making and designing stuff, until they get so knocked back by the failures that they stop trying. If you are there to slow things down a bit at the planning stage, come up with some materials which actually work (children's glue doesn't stick; children's scissors don't cut), lend a helping hand when it's needed but be sensitive enough to back out when it isn't, then you're probably doing everything you should already.

The other thing to do is to let your child help you when you are tackling a practical problem. Whether you're designing a gadget to keep the squirrels away from the bird table, trying to find a way to stop the towels falling off the towel rail onto the floor or creating a birthday cake in the shape of a penguin, enlist your child's help. Let him make his suggestions and see if they work. The combination of his imagination and your know-how may be one that makes you both succeed beyond your wildest expectations.

Information and Communication Technology (ICT)

Your child belongs to the electronic age. The chances are that she will become far more technically competent than you ever are, and will continue to develop new skills throughout her life, as the new technologies develop. Be that as it may, even space-age-children need to start somewhere, and to learn the basics. In KS1 much of this is about familiarity with information and communication technology, and with the need to develop confidence in using it.

One of the great gifts of the modern age is how easy it is, now, to find things out. In the 'old days' the teacher was the repository of knowledge, aided by a few well-chosen books. Now, most of the facts of the world are available more or less instantly. Children throughout KS1 are encouraged to explore the best ways of finding things out. Clearly, this may well involve technology, and they are encouraged to use this, but it may also involve more than they think. In a world where the obvious answer to a question is to "Google it", it may take some support for children to realise that there are other ways to find things out. If you want to know the facts of what it was like in a mine in the 1940s then the computer will, indeed give you a wealth of information. On the other hand, using books or DVDs, visiting a mine or talking to people who worked in one will all give you as good, and perhaps better, understanding of the subject. Children are encouraged to consider a number of sources when they want to find something out.

They are also supported in the best ways to store information. They are taught the basics of databases, and about how best to both store and retrieve information. They also learn about the various ways in which information can be shared.

They are encouraged to use the technology that is available to them to develop their ideas. A drawing may still be a good way to illustrate what they are writing, but so is a photograph, a diagram, a map or a chart. They need to explore how to use technology and to 'try things out'. They need to be able to review what they have done, understand what happened, perhaps explain what went wrong. They need to explore the most effective ways of presenting what they learn. Should they print work out, or would a slide-show or a presentation be more effective?

By KS2 the children may be becoming quite sophisticated users of communication technology (although it is important to be aware that this is likely to vary from child to child, depending perhaps on the degree to which they see their parents using this technology at home.) Many children are proficient at computer games, but they may still need to be supported to see that communication technology is a great deal more than that. They need to learn how modern communication technology can support them in all areas of the curriculum including finding information, communication ideas effectively, checking for accuracy and helping with organisation. They need to be aware of both the huge advantages which information and communication technology brings, and also to be aware of its limitations.

How to help at home

ICT is an area where the amount, and type, of support at home can make a great difference. Unfortunately this is not really fair: children do not all operate on the same 'level playing field.' Some have parents who have all the latest ICT equipment, and the knowledge of how to use it. Children of these parents will see their parents using ICT routinely in their daily lives, and are aware of how ICT is developing all the time. Such children are likely to become proficient with ICT almost without realising it. They may have many of the technologies themselves, and have access to others. They may send texts, email, use messaging, access the internet, play games on-line and so on routinely, and find it puzzling that everyone does not do so. Other children have parents who are far less confident in this area. They may not have a computer at home, or if they do may not have parents who are at home with it. As well as all the differences of income, background, beliefs and education, differences in attitude can also be great. For some families the computer is as central as the telephone had become ten years ago. For others it is essentially alien.

It would be crass to suggest that, to help their children, all parents should go out and buy a computer, and attend classes on how to use it. Children are, anyway, becoming familiar with technology and technology is moving on so quickly that most will outstrip their parents' knowledge (at whatever level that may be) very quickly.

Perhaps the best way for all parents to support their children at home with ICT is to keep talking to them. Stay aware of what the child is doing, and keep reinforcing safety guidelines. All of us are likely to find, in the next few years, that our children are talking about a world of which we know little. If we let them teach us about it, at least there is a chance we can all stay in touch!

History

History, as a subject, is one with which most of us are far more familiar. 'Ah, yes', we say. 'We did this at school...' Although this is true, things have nonetheless moved on a little.

History is still about the past, and about learning what happened there. It is now, though, rather more about looking at *how* we know, about evaluating sources and questioning attitudes and conclusions, and about exploring both the reasons for what happened and the effects of what happened on modern times.

In KS1 children first learn about what the past is (and when it happened!). In other words, they begin to explore chronology. They learn that their grandparents may have seen the invention of the television, but they didn't see the Romans and they certainly didn't see the dinosaurs! They are encouraged also to ask questions, not just about what happened in the past, but about why it happened. They begin to understand that one event sparked another, and that the past is linked to the present.

In KS1 children look at their own pasts, and understand that they are changing. They are encouraged to expand this to realising that change is happening all around. They are encouraged to find out what was different when their parents and grandparents were their age. They look also at the way people lived in the more distant past, and at the way inventions, explorers, rulers or scientists have influenced the past and changed history. They look at specific events in history (depending on what anniversaries local, national or international may be occurring at the time) and at what happened at this time and why.

As they move into KS2 the children's understanding of history should become more secure and they should be able to place events more accurately in context with each other. Their vocabulary should become more sophisticated, and they should be able to use the language of time ('ancient and modern', 'BC and AD', 'century, decade and millennium' and so on.) They begin to be able to identify the characteristic features of various historical periods and indeed to predict what life would have been like at that time. They begin to be able to empathise to some extent what the lives of men, women and children may have been like in the past. They begin to understand the huge range of human experience, and to understand that what they take as 'normal' is not the only experience of life, either in the past or currently. They begin to have an awareness of the huge diversity of physical, cultural, religious and ethnic experience of societies past and present.

They also begin to understand that the way history is presented is open to interpretation. The Romans' view of the building of Hadrian's Wall may not be the same as the Celts' view. This ability to understand that there is no such thing as a totally neutral account of the past (in other words the concept of historical bias) is something which they will continue to explore into KS3 and beyond.

During KS2 most children will undertake a local history study to do with their own environment, and a wider historical study to do with British history.

In their wider study they may look at the Greeks and the influence of the Greek civilisation on the ancient world, at the Romans, Anglo-Saxons and Vikings in Britain, and at the Tudors and the world in Tudor times. They may also undertake a study of either Victorian Britain or Britain since 1930, and a study of the everyday lives of men, women and children in a past society (for example that of Ancient Egypt, Ancient Sumer, the Assyrian Empire, the Indus Valley, the Maya, Benin or the Aztecs.)

How to help at home

The best way to help your child with history is to awaken an interest in the past. Tell your child about how it was when you were young. He may not be able to comprehend a world without the computer, let alone without mobile phones, 24 hour television, microwaves and so on. If you have older relatives, they too can give a window into an even more unfamiliar world. You could allow your child to experience something of what these other worlds were like. Could you manage an evening without electricity? What will you do? How will you eat? How will you keep warm? Lighting a candle and ascending into the pitch-dark upstairs can be enough to awaken the imagination of most children (not to say to terrify them!)

You are also in a position to help your child get the past into some sort of order in her head. When things happened, how long ago the various parts of the past were – these are difficult concepts for children to grasp. When a child is very young, 'yesterday' may be hardly real (since it is not 'now'), and a past from before she was born may be a real mystery. You are in a position to help here as you share your child's personal past. You are in a position to expand that understanding to include the fact that, when your child was a baby, you too were younger. Perhaps Great Uncle George was still alive, or you still had Patch the Jack Russell. You can show your child photographs, and you have her real, personal past at your fingertips to use to help her explore this difficult concept.

You can also, of course, take advantage of the huge range of resources that we have all around us. Museums, remembered from our childhood as rather dry, dull places, are now usually interactive, stimulating and exciting places to visit. Heritage Centres have been set up at all sorts of places to allow the public to experience the past. Many of these have the opportunity to dress up in the clothes of the day, eat historically accurate food, have a go at making the relevant crafts.

There is a wealth of great days out, wherever in the country you happen to live, where most of the work of making history interesting has been done for you. All you have to do is pack the sandwiches and take yourselves along…

Finally there are all sorts of books, television programmes and films that can spark a child's interest in the past.

Read a good historical children's book to your child then visit the place where it was set. Hire a DVD of a film on the subject and watch it together. The whole of the events of the world to the present day are 'history'; there is so much for you to explore with your child, and it can be so much fun!

Geography

If history is a subject that it is easy to see as interesting and exciting to explore with your child, geography is one that may provoke a slight sigh. It is not, immediately, as inspiring!

That said, it is a wider and more diverse subject than we may have found it when we were at school. It is about our environment – about our world – and about how it is changing and our effect on it. As such, it is a very relevant subject for the modern child.

In KS1 children begin to develop an awareness of geography, or rather of place. They are encouraged to ask questions about where they live, for example, why has the school got a fence around it? Why is there a pedestrian crossing opposite? What do the zig-zags mean on the road outside the school? To help them, the children are supported to observe, to look and to record what they see. In recording, they are gradually introduced to the concepts of plans, maps and the globe.

In understanding the place they see around them, they are encouraged to compare and contrast it to other places, both a real environment which they might visit and other places in the world which they learn about through books, films, photographs or the internet. They learn to observe what occurs in nature and what has been the result of intervention by people. They begin to appreciate the influence which humans have on their environment, and to recognise the need to improve and sustain that environment.

By KS2 this understanding has developed to the point where they are able to ask relevant questions about why an environment is as it is, and what can be done to sustain or to change it. They become more sophisticated in their ability to carry out fieldwork, to observe accurately and to record what they observe. They begin to understand that geography – place – may be dependent on different people's wishes, and to appreciate that different people make different demands on the environment. They may, for example, be able to understand and contribute to the various arguments about the building of a road to by-pass their town.

In a wider way, they may begin to understand that there may be similar diverse viewpoints on national, international or global issues. They may, for example, investigate the impact of 'food miles', or the arguments for and against the increased planting of crops for Bio-fuels. They are likely to explore different ways of presenting their arguments, and the information they have collected, including the use of ICT.

In the course of the key stage they are likely to explore a locality in the United Kingdom and one in a country which is less economically developed. They may explore themes such as water and its effect on landscapes and people, how settlements differ and change and an environmental issue, either local, global or both.

How to help at home

Much though it may irritate us to have our children dictate our shopping habits, our recycling responsibilities, our choice of light-bulbs or our use of the tumble-drier, the greater awareness of young people in our society of the effects of what we do on our environment must still be seen as a positive thing. This greater awareness makes geography a far more vibrant subject for many children, and can help us to see things with new eyes. When you are out and about with your child, ask her questions about what you see around her and encourage her to ask you. You may not know all the answers, but the increased awareness is useful nonetheless. Discuss the rating for the new fridge freezer; remember to take your shopping basket to avoid having to use plastic bags; discuss together the various considerations about a holiday destination; discuss the packaging of food. Can your daughter guess where the strawberries in the supermarket have come from? Does she know where that is? Could she find it on a map or globe? How much has it cost the environment to get them here? Is she willing to go without strawberries until they are in season at the local 'pick-your-own'? Greater awareness of our place on this planet, and our effect on it, may be uncomfortable, but it does have huge relevance. Explore that planet with your child.

We often take our familiarity with our world for granted. Look at an atlas together; trace the travels of a friend or relative; explore where the tea from your tea bags originated. Geography is about this fragile planet of ours, and we (all of us) need the next generation to take on responsibility for it. This is a good place to start!

Art and Design

Art and Design, together with what might have been called in the old days 'craft', are about the child's ability to be creative and imaginative. This may be through the observation of the world around them – drawing, painting or modelling what they see – or through expressing the world in their imagination, inspired by the work of other artists (local or international, contemporary or classic), by nature, by ideas, poetry...or any other stimuli which fires them up. It is about producing work in visual form, but also about producing work that may be tactile, which may involve use of colour, of pattern, line, tone, form or texture. It may involve working by themselves on individual projects, or collaboratively on larger group projects. It involves evaluating what they and others have done, and beginning to form an ability to make critical judgements based on understanding, knowledge and preference.

How to help at home

Some parents find this easy and natural ...and others find it a torture! If you are the sort of parent who has encouraged finger-paining from an early age, glued pieces of pasta to make flowers or painted a design on the side of the tool shed, you won't have a problem in encouraging Art and Design. You may delight in developing your child's skill, encourage work on huge projects, try out different media and generally throw yourself into the whole subject with glee. One of the wonders of having a child, for some people, is this second chance to have a go at drawing, colouring in, painting, modelling, building with papier mache, making junk models and generally having a chance to express themselves in a way they probably wouldn't dare if their child didn't give them the excuse. For these people, helping at home is second nature.

For others, the idea of 'expressing themselves' artistically makes them faint at the knees – as does the horror of the mess that it is going to produce in their kitchen. If this is you, do not despair! There are plenty of clubs and classes around which you can go along to with your child, and plenty of others at which your artistically-interested child can be left on her own. Most out-of-school provision has an element of large craft, so this is always a possibility, as are Beavers, Cubs, Scouts, Rainbows, Brownies and Guides. If this is not your thing, in other words, you can still provide encouragement, and enthusiastic appreciation of what is produced. After all, there is, arguably, as much positive parental input in buying a frame and putting your child's work on the wall as there is in getting paint on your hands yourself.

Music

Children in KS1 mostly still retain the uninhibited pleasure in making and responding to music that many of us lose as we get older. At this age they are likely to be encouraged to sing, and to enjoy trying out different techniques in singing, from exploring rhythm to experimenting with pitch, dynamics, tempo and volume. They are also likely to have the chance to play various percussion instruments, and to 'have a go' at a wider variety of tuned instruments.

As they get older, pupils are encouraged to develop their skills through deciding on a more controlled sound. They may explore singing in parts, accompanying with a wide variety of instruments, improvising and composing using various media including ICT and listening to a wide variety of music with understanding. They will learn to work alone, in pairs, in small groups and in large groups, and to understand how different musical input can be made to work together. They are likely to be given opportunities to listen to a range of music, both live and recorded, and to be helped to make a response to it.

How to help at home

Clearly, if you can play an instrument, or if you are a singer, or can read music or otherwise have music central in your life, you are in a stronger position to help your child than if you never consider music. If you have a skill already it may be natural to want to share that. It may be that you consider music important to the extent that you are keen to play for instrument tuition for your child. This is likely to help quite considerably with your child's mastery of the skills of music.

On the other hand, if you do not consider yourself musical, there is still much you can do to share music with your child. Most of us sing to, or chant to, our babies, since it helps them to get to sleep (...and if you remember that time, you will do *anything* at that stage for sleep!) We should fight against our own self-consciousness as they get older. Singing and chanting remain great ways to interact with our children, and many children are helped to learn through using rhythm. Try clapping to a rhythm or a beat, playing the air drums, clicking your fingers, sharing 'repeat after me' songs... All are great fun and help your child to 'loosen up' around music.

Indeed, as with Art and Design, the fact that you may not have any particular music skill need not hold back your child if he has a keen interest in music. Although some of the great musicians of the world have come from musical families, many others have not. The school will be ideally placed to spark the interest that may grow into a flame of enthusiasm in your child. If this is the case, your job is to support and to encourage – and not to cover your ears as your child explores his musical enthusiasm. 'Music' can be many things, and what is sweet to his ears may sound a cacophony to you.

A lot of encouragement (and the discreet use of a firmly shut kitchen door) may be the answer.

Physical Education (PE)

With the need for an active and healthy lifestyle very much in the news these days, PE is an important subject. Through it, in school, children learn to develop their movement and physical skills, to develop a concept of both teamwork and competition and to understand what they can and cannot do with their physical bodies.

In KS1 this is about developing and acquiring basic skills, including those of balance, rolling, being still, jumping, turning, running, hopping etc. They explore Physical Education through dance activities, games activities and gymnastic activities. In KS2 this is expanded to include in addition at least two of athletics, outdoor and adventure activities and swimming.

How to help at home

As you will see from this, it is not a statutory requirement that your child be taught to swim at school.

Given this, you may feel that it is your responsibility to make sure that your child does learn to swim. Being able to manage 25 metres in the water is generally taken to be the minimum a child should achieve for safety. Otherwise, your child will be given a range of opportunities in school to both take part in physical activities and to learn about, acquire and develop skills in various physical activities. She will also be given plenty of opportunity to 'let off steam'. Most schools aim for formal PE of at least 2 hours per week, plus encouraging active playtimes. As a parent it is likely that you will want to encourage the development of at least some of these skills and enthusiasms. You may play catch with your child in the garden, buy a jumbo trampoline, go swimming each week as a family, teach your child to ride a bike, go walking on holiday, spin the rope for your child to skip. You may find that you get involved in these activities at school, perhaps by becoming a parent helper for the football team or by helping to organise one of the events at school sports day. It is perhaps a cliché, but may nevertheless be true, that the best way to help your child stay active is to be active yourself. The best way to help your child with PE at school is to model for him both how much fun a sport can be and how much benefit it can have.

****

Chapter 6

Non-Statutory Subjects

The following subjects are 'non statutory', and as such may (or may not) be tackled by different schools in different ways. There follows a very brief description of what your child is likely to meet in each subject. However, as they are not statuary in the national curriculum, in order to get a clearer idea of how your child's school is approaching each individual subject you would probably do best to approach the school directly and discuss it with them.

Religious Education

In primary schools in England children learn about Christianity and about other principal religions. They are introduced to a range of stories and artefacts from different religions, and learn about the different beliefs which people have about God. They are encouraged to recognise and to respect the importance that belief in God may have for some people. They are encouraged to explore what is important to them and to reflect on their own feelings and experiences.

By KS2 they should begin to appreciate the impact which religious belief has locally, nationally and globally. They begin to make connections between the different religions and to explore both similarities and differences between them. They are encouraged to communicate their ideas and beliefs, and to recognise and value the viewpoint of other people. They explore their own beliefs in the context of what they have learned about different religions.

Sex Education

All primary schools must provide a policy on sex education. This should be in the form of a written statement, and should be freely available to both parents and pupils.

Parents are free to withdraw their child from all or part of the school's sex education lessons.

Personal, Social and Health Education (PSHE) and Citizenship

In PSHE and Citizenship children learn about themselves as growing and changing individuals and as members of their communities. This might involve understanding the basic rules which operate in the society of school (taking turns, sharing, resisting bullying, using appropriate language and so on) and using what they learn as guidelines when they need to resolve disputes. They learn to become active members of the society of the school, taking on responsibilities and accepting the consequences of their actions. This extends, gradually, to an understanding of their place in the wider community around them and to an awareness of political and social issues locally, nationally and globally.

Modern Foreign Language

The government has made a commitment to the introduction language learning for every pupil throughout KS2 by 2010. In learning a modern foreign language at this age children have the opportunity to develop skills which lay a firm foundation for future learning. Introduction to a language gives them a raised awareness of the multi-lingual and multi-cultural world around them and gives an international dimension to their learning.

The school will choose which language or languages are available, and will decide also at what age the language should be introduced. When it is, pupils will be encouraged to both listen to and respond to oral commands and questions, to name familiar objects and items and to become familiar with common conversational phrases. They may be introduced, gradually, to the written word in the language and be encouraged to copy or compose short sentences or phrases.

****

Chapter 7

So What Are These SATS?

SATS tests (Standard Assessment Tests) take place in primary schools towards the end of KS1 (in May of Year 2 when your child is likely to be age 7) and again towards the end of KS2 (in May of Year 6 when your child is likely to be age 11). Your child is tested in English, Maths and Science – through teacher assessment at KS1 and through more formal testing at KS2. The idea of SATS is both for you to know where your child is performing as against a national average, and for the school's results at both Key Stages to be transparent.

Most children at age 7 will achieve a level 2, and most children at age 11 will achieve a level 4. The usual range available to children at KS1 is between levels 1 and 3, and at KS2 between levels 2 and 5. This level may be further divided into bands 'a', 'b'. and 'c' in order to give a more accurate account of where, within a level, the child is performing. Therefore, at age 7, level 2 might be subdivided into 2c (at the lower end of level 2), 2b (in the middle of level 2) and 2a (at the upper end of level 2). At age 11, the same subdivisions may be given for level 4 (4c at the lower end, 4b for the middle of the range and 4a at the upper end of the level). The highest level that the majority of children can achieve at KS1 is level 3 and at KS2 is level 5. Only in exceptional circumstances would provision be made to test higher than that. The lower levels that are usual for the ages are level 1 for age 7 and level 2 for age 11. Achievement below these levels (i.e. 'W', which means 'working towards level 1, at KS1, or 'W' or level 1 at KS2) is likely to mean that your child is underachieving significantly in that subject and will need extra help.

SATS results are designed also to help you monitor how your child is progressing against his or her own previous performance. These results are sometimes expressed as a number, and are 'age standardised'. For this the mean (average) score is set at 100, with a standard deviation of 15. Your child is therefore performing at the exact average for his age if he scores 100, and most children can expect to score between 85 and 115. These scores are age-adjusted, so may be compared year to year. In other words, if your daughter scored 102 last year, you would hope she would score 102 this year, if she is doing as well.

As a rough benchmark, with the Attainment Level results, you would hope that your child would progress two levels between each set of national tests. If he obtained a level 2 at KS1 you would hope he would achieve a level 4 at KS2. However, this can be slightly misleading. Therefore, if he achieved a level 3 at KS1, this may in fact have been a level 3c.

Progression to 4a in these circumstances is a good result, even though it may appear he has only gone up one attainment level.

SATS results are issued before the end of the summer term. This means they are available to the KS2 class teacher, and can also be used at a change of school to Secondary to give an indication of how the child can be expected to work in KS3. They are, however, really an 'internal' measure designed to help you, your child and your child's teacher. At the end of KS4, when your child is 16, he will take the first of the National qualifications (GCSEs and so on) which are the first 'external' results that he is likely to take with him into adult life.

Chapter 8

What Do Our Children Learn?

This may seem a redundant question with which to finish this book. After all, hasn't the whole book been describing just that?

The philosophy behind the question is that learning cannot, however helpful it might be for us to describe it as such, be quantified into neat bundles. Yes, we can describe how well a pupil has absorbed facts about science or how well he can he write a story – but most learning goes across subject boundaries. More than that, learning as part of developing and growing-up is impossible to quantify. We all learn, all the time. However hard we try, we cannot package how much of that learning should happen between the hours of 9am and 3.30pm, Monday to Friday in term time.

For one thing, some skills do not fall neatly into curriculum subjects. Writing comes under literacy – but the ability to write fluently, persuasively, articulately and with clarity is needed across all areas of the curriculum. Without the ability to read and understand or interpret what is read, the knowledge gained by others in the world may not be available to a pupil. If a pupil cannot listen to what is taught, and communicate his own ideas and responses, he

111

will not be able to make the most of the school curriculum, or wider life experiences. Similarly, numbers occur in a great many areas other than in maths, and technology is all around us and not confined to a timetabled slot called 'ICT'. Children's learning is all joined up, and advances in one area should prompt and promote advances in another. More worryingly, a weakness in one area can have an effect across the whole curriculum, so that a child who has difficulty in a quite specific area may find his progress generally slowed, unless he is given support to prevent this.

Schools are very good, these days, about being alert for all sorts of conditions from dyslexia to deafness, from something as simple as not being able to see the white-board to something as complex as autism spectrum conditions. That said, you as parents know your child best, and it is always worth spending the time to question why your child may be doing less well at school than you might expect. The reason may not be immediately clear. A child who is struggling is likely to enjoy lessons less, and perhaps to express this as 'not liking' the class teacher. Often when a child does less well one year than the last, parents accept the idea that it is the class teacher this year who is at fault, without checking behind this to make sure there isn't an underlying issue with their child. What is certain is that, with any issue affecting your child's progress and happiness, the earlier it can be identified and remedied the better so it always worth pursuing any concerns which you might have.

Some areas of learning are so broad that it is impossible to even consider them under a specific curriculum subject heading. They include areas such as problem-solving skills and the ability to persevere with a problem and approach it in different ways. They include being able to work with other people and also being able to work independently and with self-motivation. They include the ability to reason, to be curious, to be creative and to look critically what they have achieved.

Many wider skills are promoted, consciously, across the curriculum in schools. For example, the ability to make sensible choices in relation to managing money – financial skills – may be tackled in various areas such as mathematics, PSHE and Citizenship and also through in-school enterprise projects. Many schools run clubs or societies, and the pupils may learn to manage the finances of these. They may also be encouraged to be involved in community and charity activities, and to come up with ways to raise money for these, together with innovative and imaginative ideas to promote them. Throughout their school experience pupils in the 21st century are being encouraged to think about the environment, to be aware of sustainable development and of the impact which we as individuals and communities can have on the world we live on.

Much of learning as children grow up is to do with making sense of the world around them. They need to develop a sense of self, of their potential and their limitations. As their understanding develops, so does their curiosity about some of the fundamental issues that face us all. They learn to develop their inner lives, their belief systems and their own answers to life's questions. They develop their understanding of right and wrong, and their appreciation of the responsibilities involved in this moral awareness. Hand in hand with this comes an awareness of their place in society, both the society of school and that of family and of the wider community. They learn to take their place in these societies, to develop a sense of belonging and responsibility towards a common good. They learn to respect both their own and other people's cultural traditions, and make their own contributions to their culture. They learn, in short, what it is to 'grow up'.

Clearly, this wider learning does not take place solely at school. School society is only one part of where they 'are', and some would argue that it is a very small, and in some ways rather artificial part. For it to be an effective part, it will work best if the society of school reflects the values that you cultivate at home and which are in the wider societies of which your child is a member. This is why the spiritual and moral ethos of the school is so important. School will teach your child a great deal more than the specific content of the various curriculum subjects, and it is important that you understand what this will be, and agree to that taking place.

Equally, it is important to the school that you support that ethos. There can be conflict between home and school when parents do not support the social and cultural rules of the school – for example, the completing of homework or the wearing of correct school uniform. Some school require a home/school contract to be signed by all three participating parties (the school, the parents and the pupil), which articulates what is being expected by each of the parties. Even if your child's school does not do this, you are entering into a partnership with the school when your child joins, and it is likely the partnership will work best if all of you are clear that you all want the same outcomes.

The journey that your child takes through the primary school years is a great one. During that time, she goes from being a child barely able to function independently – needing help with dressing, personal hygiene, eating, communicating and much more – to a person on the verge of adulthood. She learns the academic skills that provide the foundation of all the learning that is to follow. She acquires a set of intellectual tools that enable her to go on, as an independent individual, to the next stage of life. She gains awareness and understanding of who she is. She develops a set of values that place her in the society around her.

During this time, you will have made the journey with your child. Seven years does not seem long in our lives, but sharing them with our child we realise just what can be accomplished in this time. When our child goes off to secondary school, we are seven years older – and possibly a little wiser. If it is true, that "education is wasted on the young", then perhaps at least it is not wasted on the young's parents. Perhaps this time round we may realise what a huge experience it all is. Enjoy it!

For further information:

http://curriculum.qca.org.uk

Copies of the national curriculum, together with
frameworks for literacy and numeracy are available free of
charge, from the Qualifications and Curriculum Authority

83 Piccadilly
London W1J 8QA
Tel: 020 7509 5555

Emerald Publishing
www.emeraldpublishing.co.uk

106 Ladysmith Road
Brighton BN2 4EG

Other titles in the Emerald Series:

Law
Guide to Bankruptcy
Conducting Your Own Court case
Guide to Consumer law
Creating a Will
Guide to Family Law
Guide to Employment Law
Guide to European Union Law
Guide to Health and Safety Law
Guide to Criminal Law
Guide to Landlord and Tenant Law
Guide to the English Legal System
Guide to Housing Law
Guide to Marriage and Divorce
Guide to The Civil Partnerships Act
Guide to The Law of Contract
The Path to Justice
You and Your Legal Rights

Health
Guide to Combating Child Obesity
Asthma Begins at Home

Music
How to Survive and Succeed in the Music Industry

General
A Practical Guide to Obtaining probate
A Practical Guide to Residential Conveyancing
Writing The Perfect CV
Keeping Books and Accounts-A Small Business Guide
Business Start Up-A Guide for New Business
Finding Asperger Syndrome in the Family-A Book of Answers

For details of the above titles published by Emerald go to:

www.emeraldpublishing.co.uk